Easy To Follow Practice Sessions For Players Ages 8 to 11

Drills and games
- easy to understand
- simple to use
- systematically organized

by
Peter Schreiner and Gerd Thissen

Illustrations:
Karlheinz Grindler

Library of Congress Cataloging - in - Publication Data

by Schreiner, Peter
    24 Easy To Follow Practice Sessions for Players Ages 8 to 11

ISBN # 1-890946-47-8
Library of Congress Catalog Number 00-105974
Copyright © July 2000

Originally published in Germany in 2000
by Rowohlt Taschenbuch Verlag GmbH.

Art Direction/Layout
Kimberly N. Bender

Illustrations
Karlheinz Grindler

Editing and Proofing
Bryan R. Beaver

Printed by
DATA REPRODUCTIONS
Auburn, Michigan

Cover Photography
EMPICS

REEDSWAIN Publishing
612 Pughtown Road • Spring City • Pennsylvania 19475
1-800-331-5191 • www.reedswain.com
EMAIL: info @reedswain.com

24

Easy To Follow Practice Sessions
For Players Ages 8 to 11

Drills and games
- easy to understand
- simple to use
- systematically organized

by
Peter Schreiner and Gerd Thissen

Illustrations:
Karlheinz Grindler

published by
REEDSWAIN Publishing

Contents

Coaching Philosophy

The coach must create **conditions that are suitable for young players,** based on the following principles and rules.

1. **Young players should not be coached simply by using trimmed-down versions of adult coaching methods!**

   - Young players should be coached by methods that are appropriate to them and can motivate them.
   - The choice of drills and the way they are explained should be tailored to the age of the young players and their level of development.
   - The coaching should be broad-based and varied.

2. **Use suitable balls**
   The balls used should be smaller and lighter than standard balls. This means that young players can practice their technique without taxing their strength and will thus enjoy more success.

3. **Simplify and modify the rules**
   Beginners need only a few basic rules. However, it is important that the coach explains these rules clearly. The coach can introduce additional rules so that the players are rewarded when they master certain techniques. For example, headed goals might count double when they are scored during a Practice Session devoted to heading technique.

4. **Reduce the number of players**
   This has the following advantages:
   - Fewer demands are made on the players' technique.
   - The game remains tactically simple.
   - All of the players are intensively involved, both physically and emotionally, because each player makes a larger contribution to the team performance.
   - All of the players are directly involved in their team's victory or defeat.
   - Each player has plenty of ball contacts and is actively involved in the game.
   - All of the players inevitably have to carry out attacking and defensive tasks. Even the weaker performers therefore have a responsible role in their team.

5. **Use smaller playing areas**
   Advantages:
   - Young players can easily take in a small playing area.
   - Young players can follow the game situations and defensive and attacking moves more easily.
   - The game takes place close to the goals, so defensive and attacking situations follow each other in rapid succession and each player has lots of goal-scoring opportunities.
   - Moreover, each player is inevitably involved in the attacking and defensive tasks of his

team.
The size of the playing area should be increased as the young players become older.

6. Make use of young players' natural enjoyment of running and playing

Young players love to run and play. Coaches should take advantage of this and give them lots of opportunities to burn off their abundant energy.
Explanations should therefore be as short as possible, so that the young players do not have to stand around for too long.

7. Put the emphasis on the ball and scoring goals

Young players experience every action that is centered around the ball as an exciting game. These situations can therefore be used to motivate them. Drills and small sided games with the emphasis on shooting at goal provide young players with lots of "success moments."

8. Allow young players to play as often and as long as they want

As many young players as possible should be able to practice and play simultaneously for the same length of time during training sessions. If they have to stand and watch, their enjoyment and enthusiasm disappear very quickly. Moreover, they can only improve by practicing and playing as often as possible.
Coaches should also ensure that all of their players, rather than just the best ones, participate in competitive matches against other teams.

9. Encourage individuals to express themselves

The performance and success of the individual should be encouraged just as much as team success. However, the coach should also be aware that, in the long term, the creativity of individual players can only bring about the desired success on the soccer pitch if the individual learns to cooperate with the other members of the team.

10. Create competitive and motivating situations

Willingness to learn and achieve are especially great when training sessions incorporate competitive situations. Drills should therefore be derived from real game situations.

11. Select typical game situations

The basic principle of the game of soccer is: Score goals and don't concede goals.
Young players can easily grasp this idea, which should be at the heart of as many drills as possible. The creation of scoring chances and the defense of the goal are basic requirements that young players can easily put into practice.

12. Take account of the differences between young players

A coach should take account of differences in skill, expectations and interests. Young players with different degrees of soccer talent, soccer experience and soccer interest should be able to find their own level. Some might simply want to play for enjoyment, while others might have the ambition to develop their soccer skills selectively and effectively.

Stretching exercises

Before the main part of each training session, young players should carry out stretching exercises to prepare themselves for the following drills.

Stretching and mobility exercises prevent injuries and ensure that young players develop and maintain the flexibility needed to play soccer.

Young players should learn at an early age that stretching exercises are a very important part of their preparation for training sessions and matches.

The following exercises are ideal preparation for the demands made on soccer players.

Exercise no. 1

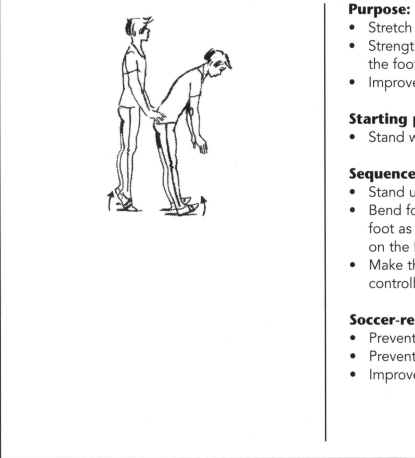

Purpose:
- Stretch and strengthen the calf muscles
- Strengthen the muscles of the front of the foot
- Improve sense of balance

Starting position:
- Stand with legs slightly apart

Sequence of movements:
- Stand up straight on tiptoe
- Bend forward, raising the front of each foot as high as possible and standing on the heels
- Make the transition in as calm and controlled a manner as possible

Soccer-related aspects:
- Prevents ankle ligament injuries
- Prevents Achilles tendon complaints
- Improves the flexibility of the ankle

Exercise no. 2

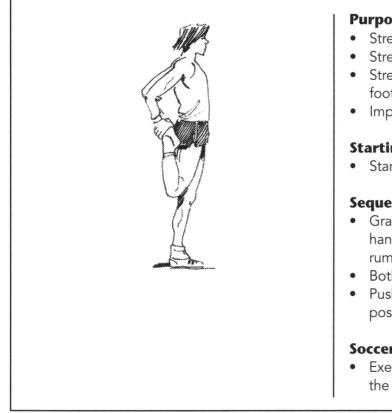

Purpose:
- Stretch the groin muscles
- Stretch the lower leg extensors
- Stretch the muscles of the front of the foot
- Improve sense of balance

Starting position:
- Stand with legs slightly apart

Sequence of movements:
- Grasp the front of the foot with both hands and pull the foot up to touch the rump.
- Both thighs should be close together
- Push the hips forward and hold this position

Soccer-related aspects:
- Exercises the muscles used in kicking with the instep

Exercise no. 3

Purpose:
- Stretch the lower leg flexors
- Stretch the muscles in the back of the leg

Starting position:
- Place one foot forward and bend the knee
- Place the heel of the back leg on the ground
- Both feet pointing forward

Sequence of movements:
- Bend the upper body forward until the hands can touch the ground
- Straighten the back leg while keeping the heel on the ground

Soccer-related aspects:
- Exercise to prevent Achilles tendon injuries

Exercise no. 4

Purpose:
- Stretch the gluteus maximus
- Stretch the groin muscles

Starting position:
- Adopt a sprint start position
- Upper body bent forward, touching the knee of the front leg

Sequence of movements:
- Place the hands to each side of the front foot as a support and bend the upper body as far forward as possible

Soccer-related aspects:
- Exercise to prevent Achilles tendon injuries

VARIATIONS:

Standing with upper body upright:
- Hold the upper body upright
- Push the hips forward
- Straighten and stretch the back leg

Soccer-related aspects:
- Exercises the muscles used in kicking with the instep

Exercise no. 5

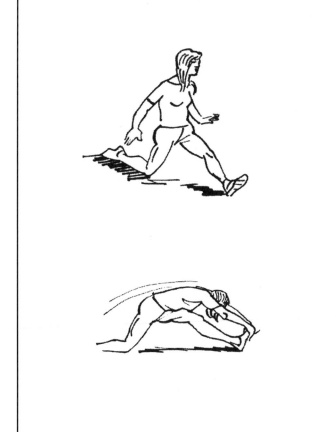

Purpose:
- Stretch the lower leg flexors
- Stretch the groin muscles

Starting position:
- Kneel on one knee
- One leg stretched forward

Sequence of movements:
- Bend the upper body forward
- Grasp the tip of the foot with both hands

Note:
- Straighten the knee
- Press the foot forward to resist the pull of the hands

Soccer-related aspects:
- Exercises the muscles used in tackling

Exercise no. 6

Purpose:
- Stretch the abductors
- Mobilization of the hip joint

Starting position:
- Sit with the soles of the feet together
- Pull the heels toward the body

Sequence of movements:
- With the elbows or the hands, press the knees down toward the ground.

Note:
- Keep the upper body upright

Soccer-related aspects:
- Exercises the muscles used in tackling
- Suitable as special exercise for goalkeepers
- Prevents groin strains (common problem among soccer players)

Exercise no. 7

Purpose:
- Stretching the abductors
- Stretching the lower leg flexors
- Stretching the gluteal muscles
- Stretching the muscles in the back of the leg
- Mobilization of the hip joint

Starting position:
- Legs wide apart
- Legs straight

Sequence of movements:
- Slowly bend the upper body forward.
- Rest the hands on the ground

Note:
- Ensure that feet cannot slip when standing with legs wide apart
- Do not bend forward suddenly
- Gradually move feet wider apart
- Be especially careful if any pain is experienced in the groin area or the hip joint

Variation 1:
- Bend the lower arms so that they are parallel to the ground and bend forward to touch the arms to the ground

Variation 2:
- Move the upper body and arms toward one leg

Soccer-related aspects:
- Exercises muscles used in tackling
- Suitable as special exercise for goalkeepers
- Prevents groin strains (common problem among soccer players)

Exercise no. 8

Purpose:
• Stretch the abductors

Starting position:
• Legs wide apart
• Both feet pointing forward

Sequence of movements:
• Bend one leg with the full sole on the ground
• Keep the other leg stretched and press against the ground
• Rest the inside edge of the foot on the ground

Note:
• Keep upper body upright
• A support aid can be used if balance problems are experienced (e.g. support by another player)

Variation:
• Move the upper body and arms toward one leg

Purpose:
• Stretch the calf muscles

Soccer-related aspects:
• Prevents groin strains (common problem among soccer players)

Practice Session no. 1
Dribbling 1

ORGANIZATION	DESCRIPTION	TIME
	Rules of the game: • Four pairs of players (A1-A2; B1-B2; ...) stand at the start. Each pair has a ball. • One player from each pair (A1, B1, C1, D1, ...) dribbles round the square. • The second player waits until his partner returns to the start cone, takes the ball and dribbles around the square. • The players count the number of rounds that they dribble in six minutes ("6 days"). • The pair with the most rounds wins. • Two sessions are played, or a day lasts 2 minutes. **Note:** This is a form of interval training, i.e. alternating periods of exertion and rest.	15
ORGANIZATION		5

A) DRIBBLING IN A STAR
 	
	Drill 1:
	• The players dribble the ball simultaneously from the outside cone toward the center cone.
	• About 1 yard before they reach the center cone they turn around and dribble the ball back to the start cone.
	
	• Techniques that can be used:
	  • Drag-back with the sole of the foot
	  • Change of direction (inside)
	  • Change of direction (outside)
		5

ORGANIZATION	DESCRIPTION	TIME

B) DRIBBLING IN A TRIANGLE
 	
	Drill 2:
	• Each player marks out a triangle with three cones and dribbles the ball from cone to cone
	• Direction of turn at the cones: left and right
	
	• Techniques that can be used:
	  • Change of direction (inside)
	  • Change of direction (outside)
	  • Rotation (inside)
		5

C) TRIANGLE WITH CENTER CONE
 	
	Drill 3:
	• Three players dribble simultaneously with a ball toward the cone in the center.
	• About 1 yard from the center cone they turn to the left and dribble to the next cone.
	• When they have all reached their outside cone, they dribble toward the center cone again.
	• Direction of turn: left and right
	• In the middle they perform a feint:
	  • Dummy step
	  • Step-over
		5

D) SQUARE WITH CENTER CONE 	**Drill 4:** • As c) in this drill, four players dribble from the corners of a square toward the cone in the center.	5

ORGANIZATION	DESCRIPTION	TIME
FINAL GAME: 4 V 4 WITH 2 GOALS 	**Points to observe:** • Keeping the ball close to the foot • Lots of dribbles • Lots of feints • Screen the ball from an opponent	35

Practice Session no. 2
Dribbling 2

ORGANIZATION	DESCRIPTION	TIME
WARMING-UP GAME: **CATCHING CLOTHS**	**Description of the game:** • The players dribble at random in a playing area measuring, for example, 15 x 15 yards. • Each player dribbles with a ball and has a cloth (handkerchief, marker band, etc.) tucked into the back of his shorts so that most of it hangs free. • All of the players try to "steal" the cloths from the other players. • They hold the stolen cloths in one hand. However, one cloth must always be tucked into the back of the shorts. • The player who steals the most cloths is the winner.	10
STRETCHING EXERCISES		5

A) ZIG-ZAG DRIBBLING
 	
STEP-OVER
 	
	Drill 1:
	• The players start at two cones and dribble in a zig-zag to the turning point and then back to the starting cones.
	• Start direction: to right and left
	• Techniques:
	  • Change of direction (inside)
	  • Change of direction (outside)
	  • Rotation (inside)
	  • Dummy step
	  • Step-over
	  • Scissor
	
	Aims:
	Lots of changes of direction and turns; improved ball control.
		20

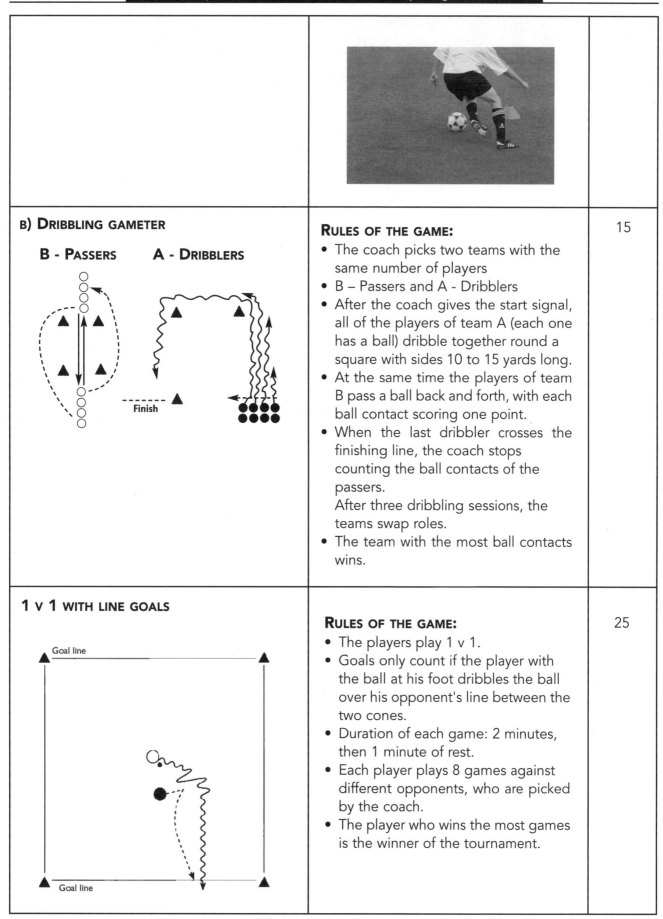

b) Dribbling gameter

B - Passers   A - Dribblers

Finish

RULES OF THE GAME:
- The coach picks two teams with the same number of players
- B – Passers and A - Dribblers
- After the coach gives the start signal, all of the players of team A (each one has a ball) dribble together round a square with sides 10 to 15 yards long.
- At the same time the players of team B pass a ball back and forth, with each ball contact scoring one point.
- When the last dribbler crosses the finishing line, the coach stops counting the ball contacts of the passers.
  After three dribbling sessions, the teams swap roles.
- The team with the most ball contacts wins.

15

1 v 1 with line goals

Goal line

Goal line

RULES OF THE GAME:
- The players play 1 v 1.
- Goals only count if the player with the ball at his foot dribbles the ball over his opponent's line between the two cones.
- Duration of each game: 2 minutes, then 1 minute of rest.
- Each player plays 8 games against different opponents, who are picked by the coach.
- The player who wins the most games is the winner of the tournament.

25

Practice Session No. 3
Dribbling 3

ORGANIZATION	DESCRIPTION	TIME
	Shadow dribbling • Two players dribble, one behind the other. • Each has a ball. • The player in front decides what direction he will dribble in and what additional movements he will make. **These additional movements are:** • stretching exercises with the ball • feints • sudden changes of direction	15
STRETCHING EXERCISES		5
A) **PAIRS** 	**Drill 1:** • A and B dribble toward each other from a distance of 10 yards apart. • When they are about 2 yards apart they dodge to the side. • The coach indicates the direction they have to dodge. • Techniques: Change of direction, dummy step, step-over, scissor • Number of repeats: 10 times to the right 10 times to the left	5

ORGANIZATION	DESCRIPTION	TIME
B) FOURS 	• Same as drill 1 • After dodging to the side, the players (A1 and B1) pass the ball to the waiting players (A2 and B2). • Techniques as in the previous drill	5
C) DRIBBLING COMPETITIONTION 	• Two players dribble over a course in competition against each other. • Who reaches the finish line first? • Which team scores the most points?	15

ORGANIZATION	DESCRIPTION	TIME
FINAL TOURNAMENT Goal line Goal line	**Rules of the game:** • This is a game of 2 v 2. • Goals only count if the player with the ball at his foot dribbles the ball over his opponents' line between the two cones. • Duration of the game: 2 minutes, then 1 minute of rest. • Each pair plays 10 games against different pairs. The pair that wins the most games is the tournament winner.	35

Practice Session no. 4
Dribbling 4

ORGANIZATION	DESCRIPTION	TIME
WARMING UP IN THE "ZIPPER" WITH BALL	**Two lines of players thread their path through each other.** **Drills with the ball** • Players on the left carry a ball – players on the right have no ball – the ball is transferred in the center • Players on the left dribble the ball – players on the right have no ball – the ball is transferred in the center • Both lines of players have a ball – players on the left carry the ball - players on the right dribble the ball - the balls are swapped in the center • Dribbling **Drills on the long side of the area (with ball):** • Throw ball in the air while running • Bounce the ball (right hand, left hand, right and left alternately) • Dribbling	15
STRETCHING EXERCISES		5

ORGANIZATION	DESCRIPTION	TIME

DRILLS IN THE "COMB"	• The players dribble through the "comb" (forward – to the center – back – forward – etc.)
	• Vary techniques:
	  • drag-back with sole of foot
	  • change of direction (inside)
	  • change of direction (outside)
	• Aim: Confidence on the ball when an opponent challenges from the side.
	• 10 times to the right
		15

STRETCHING EXERCISES		5
DRILLS IN THE "COMB"	• A dribbles toward the center cone. • B challenges from the right. • A turns his back to B and drags the ball back. • When both players are again at their start cones, they repeat the drill. **Variation:** • B challenges from the left. • A makes a clockwise turn and dribbles back to his start cone. After 5 repeats to the left and right the players swap roles. A now becomes the defender and B dribbles.	5 5

ORGANIZATION	DESCRIPTION	TIME
DRIBBLING AND SHOOTING	• The players dribble and turn and finish with a shot at goal. • The coach or another player stands at the final cone and challenges half-heartedly, so that the players can experience a success moment and finish with a good shot at goal.	15
LINE DRIBBLE GAME	**Rules of the game:** • The players are divided into two teams of 8. • The playing area measures 20 x 40 yards. • The goal line is the line between the cones marking the end of the playing area. • A goal is scored when a player dribbles over the opposition's goal line. • Shooting over the goal line is not allowed.	30

Practice Session no. 5
Passing 1

ORGANIZATION	DESCRIPTION	TIME
WARMING UP IN THE "ZIPPER" WITHOUT A BALL: 	The players start at two cones, progress to the next cone, turn and run diagonally across the square to the opposite cone. **Activities on the long side of the square:** • Hop • Sidestep • Skip **Drills in the diagonal:** • Players in the two lines cross the middle alternately • Make complete turn just before the middle • Slap hands **Note:** The "zipper" teaches the players how to adjust their speed to the speed of their teammates.	15
STRETCHING EXERCISES		5
PASSING WITH THE INSIDE OF THE FOOT 	**Technique:** • Knee of standing leg slightly bent, with foot close to the ball • Front of foot pointing in direction of pass • Turn passing foot outward • Lean the upper body forward over the ball • Strike the ball centrally with the inside of the foot	

ORGANIZATION	DESCRIPTION	TIME
DRILLS FOR PAIRS OF PLAYERS: 	**Drill:** • A and B stand 5 to 10 yards apart • Midway between them is a goal 1 to 2 yards wide. • A sidefoots the stationary ball from a stationary position through the goal to B. • B stops the ball with the inside of his foot and sidefoots it back through the goal to A. **Notes:** • The players make eye contact before passing. • Narrow the goal when the players can pass accurately. • Increase the passing rate. • Increase the distance between the players. • Practice passing with left and right foot!	10
PASSING WHILE ON THE MOVE	**Setup as above** • The players take a short run-up before sidefooting the ball.	5
COMING TO MEET THE BALL 	• A and B stand 10 to 15 yards apart. • A sidefoots the ball to B. • B runs to meet the ball and sidefoots the rolling ball back along the ground. • A stops the ball – at the same time B runs back to his starting position. **Note:** • Gradually increase the distance between the two players.	5

ORGANIZATION	DESCRIPTION	TIME
D) VARYING THE DISTANCE 	• A and B sidefoot the ball back and forth while on the move. • They vary their distance apart as shown in the drawing from 2-3 yards to 10-12 yards.	5
CONE SHOOTING 	• Three teams are formed. • Team A plays against team B and the team C players distribute themselves around the perimeter of the pitch so that they can return the balls to the other players. • The players try to hit the cones (1 point for the team). • The players must not cross the line before shooting. • The game ends when all of the cones have been hit.	30

Practice Session no. 6
Passing 2

ORGANIZATION	DESCRIPTION	TIME
TARGETED THROW-INS	• The players take throw-ins, trying to hit the players on the other side of the neutral zone. • Each hit scores one point. • If a player catches the ball, this does not count as a hit. • A hit does not count if the ball touches the ground first. • The coach counts the hits and decides who has won.	15
STRETCHING EXERCISES		5
PASSING ON THE TURN – 1 BALL	**Drill:** • A sidefoots the ball alternately to right and left. • B runs to the ball from the side and sidefoots it back with his right and left foot alternately	10

ORGANIZATION	DESCRIPTION	TIME
PASSING ON THE TURN – 2 BALLS **PASSING ON THE TURN WHILE RUNNING** 	**Drill:** • A and B stand diagonally opposite to each other. • Each sidefoots the ball forward and then turns through 90 degrees and runs to meet the ball that the other has played. • They then simultaneously sidefoot the balls back. **Note:** • The players make eye contact before sidefooting the ball forward • The players stand 4 to 6 yards apart and run forward in parallel. • They sidefoot the ball over the ground to each other as they run.	10
PASSING WITH THE INSIDE OF THE FOOT IN A TRIANGLE 	**Drill:** • The players stand at equal distances from each other in a triangle (3 to 5 yards apart). • They sidefoot the moving ball along the ground around the triangle. • Passing sequence: clockwise and counterclockwise	5

ORGANIZATION	DESCRIPTION	TIME
GAME WITH FOUR GOALS 	**Rules of the game:** • Each team (5 – 7 players) defends two goals. **Note:** This game teaches the players to use all of the available space and to switch quickly from one side to the other.	30

Practice Session no. 7
Passing 3

ORGANIZATION	DESCRIPTION	TIME
SIMON SAYS "DRIBBLE!" **SIMON SAYS "MAKE A BRIDGE"** **SIMON SAYS "CIRCLE"**	**Rules:** Each player has a ball. The playing area measures 20 x 20 yards. **The coach calls out the following commands:** • "Simon says dribble" (dribble) • "Simon says stop" (stand still with the ball at your feet) • "Simon says make a bridge" (bend forward and place both hands on the ball) • "Simon says hands up" (stand with your hands up holding the ball) • "Simon says circle" (take the ball in a circle round your hips) When the coach says "Simon says" the players have to react appropriately. If the coach just calls out "Stop!" the players continue what they are doing, because the words "Simon says" are missing. Initially none of the players has to drop out, because they have to learn the commands. Subsequently a player who carries out the wrong command or does not react correctly has to drop out.	15
STRETCHING EXERCISES		5

ORGANIZATION	DESCRIPTION	TIME
CONTINUOUS PASSING 	• A and B stand behind each other and C stands opposite them. • A sidefoots the ball along the ground to C and runs after the ball. • C runs to meet the ball and sidefoots the rolling ball to B. • B sidefoots the rolling ball to A, who has now taken up the position of C. **Note:** • The greater the distance between the players, the faster they have to sprint to the other side. • The coach can place cones as orientation aids.	10
B) TURNING AND SIDEFOOTING THE BALL 	• A and B stand 5 to 10 yards apart, each with a ball. • C stands midway between them • They pass alternately to C, who turns to face one then the other and sidefoots the ball back.	10
C) ONE-TWO WITH A NEUTRAL PLAYER 	• A player runs a short distance with the ball and passes it to a neutral player. • The neutral player passes the ball back into his path. • The player dribbles the ball on and passes to the next player, who repeats the sequence in the opposite direction, etc.	10

ORGANIZATION	DESCRIPTION	TIME
SHOOTING AT GOAL (GROUP OF 3 PLAYERS)	**Rules of the game:** • The coach divides the players into groups of three. • One player starts as goalkeeper and the other two are the strikers. • They shoot alternately at the goal, which is midway between them. • The goalkeeper turns to face one striker then the other. • If the goalkeeper stops a shot, the striker tries to score from the rebound. • After 10 shots the players swap roles. • Each player goes into goal once. • Who scores the most goals? • When all of the groups have finished, the coach organizes the players into new groups of three.	30

Practice Session no. 8
Controlling and turning with the ball 1

ORGANIZATION	DESCRIPTION	TIME
HARES AND HUNTERS 	**Rules of the game:** • The players are in a marked playing area. • 1 to 3 hunters have a ball (preferably a soft ball!). • The other players are hares. • The hunters throw the ball at the hares. When a hare is hit by the ball he picks it up and becomes a hunter. **Variation:** The hunters try to catch all of the hares as quickly as possible by hitting them all with the ball. The group that catches all of the hares fastest is the winner.	15
STRETCHING EXERCISES		5
CONTROLLING AND TURNING WITH THE BALL (INSIDE OF THE FOOT, CHANGE OF DIRECTION THROUGH 90 DEGREES) 	**Drill for groups of two players:** • Player B passes to A. • A controls the ball with the inside of the foot and turns through 90 degrees with it. • A then passes to B, who controls the ball and runs with it. **Important:** The player who receives the pass should come to meet the ball rather than waiting until it reaches him.	10

ORGANIZATION	DESCRIPTION	TIME
CONTROLLING AND TURNING WITH THE BALL (INSIDE OF THE FOOT, CHANGE OF DIRECTION THROUGH 180 DEGREES) 	**Drill for groups of three players:** • A, B and C stand 8 yards apart on a line. • Player A passes the ball along the ground to B. • B comes to meet the ball, controls it with the inside of his foot and turns through 180 degrees with the ball. • B passes to C, who passes back to B.	10
NUMBERS GAME 	• The players of a group of 5 players are given numbers from 1 to 5. Player 1 has the ball. • The players move freely around the playing area. • Player 1 passes to 2, 2 controls the ball as he runs and then passes to 3, who passes to 4, who passes to 5, who passes to 1, etc.	10
FINAL GAME **8 V 8 WITH TWO GOALS**	**Points to observe:** • Confident control of the ball and turning and running with it. • Lots of short passes – as many players as possible should be involved in the build-up of the attacks.	30

CONTROLLING AND TURNING WITH THE BALL (INSIDE OF THE FOOT):

Practice Session no. 9
Controlling and turning with the ball 2

ORGANIZATION	DESCRIPTION	TIME
	Double passes through small goals	15
	• 5 to 7 small goals are set up on the playing area.	
	• Each pair of players has one ball.	
	• Each pair chooses a goal and one player passes the ball through the goal to his partner.	
	• The partner passes the ball back immediately (first touch).	
	• This drill warms the players up and improves their ability to play a one-two.	
STRETCHING EXERCISES		5
CONTROLLING AND TURNING WITH THE BALL (OUTSIDE OF THE FOOT):	**Drill for groups of two:**	10
	• A and B stand 3 to 5 yards apart.	
	• B passes the ball to A.	
	• A controls the ball with the outside of his foot and turns through 90 degrees.	
	• A passes back to B.	
	• This is repeated 9 times, then the players swap roles.	
	IMPORTANT: The player who receives the pass should come to meet the ball rather than waiting until it reaches him.	

ORGANIZATION	DESCRIPTION	TIME
CONTROLLING THE BALL AND TURNING THROUGH 90 DEGREES: 	• B passes to A, who runs to meet the ball. • A controls the ball with the outside of the foot and turns through 90 degrees with the ball. • A dribbles round the cone and back to his starting point and passes the ball back to B. • This is repeated 9 times, then the players swap roles.	10
CONTROLLING THE BALL AND TURNING 	• A and B stand 5 to 7 yards apart. • B passes to A (1). • A runs to meet the ball, controls it with the outside of the foot and turns through 180 degrees with it. • He dribbles round the cone (2). • A passes back to B and runs back to his cone. • This is repeated 9 times, then the players swap roles.	10
TOURNAMENT: 4 V 4 WITH TWO GOALS **CONTROLLING AND TURNING WITH THE BALL (OUTSIDE OF THE FOOT):** 	**Points to observe:** • Short-passing game with confident control of the ball (especially with the outside of the foot) and turning and running with the ball • Get into a shooting position quickly	30

Practice Session no. 10
Juggling 1 – Basic Drills

ORGANIZATION	DESCRIPTION	TIME
THREE AGAINST	• Three "outside" players pass the ball accurately to each other so that the "inside" player cannot touch it. • The inside player tries to touch the ball, watching for a mistake by one of the outside players. • If the inside player touches the ball, he swaps places with one of the outside players. **Note:** The outside players are constantly in motion between the cones and the player in possession, giving him two options for passing the ball.	15
STRETCHING EXERCISES		5
A B	**Drill 1:** • The player allows the ball to fall from his hands or throws it up into the air. • He kicks the ball up into the air with his instep before it touches the ground, and catches it again. • Number of repeats: 10 times with the right foot 10 times with the left foot 10 times with right and left alternately **Drill 2:** • The player drops the ball and knocks it into the air with his thigh and catches it again. • Number of repeats: 10 times with the right thigh 10 times with the left thigh 10 times with right and left alternately	10

ORGANIZATION	DESCRIPTION	TIME
	Drill 3: • The player throws the ball up, knocks it up with his thigh as it falls again, and catches it. • Number of repeats: 10 times with the right thigh 10 times with the left thigh 10 times with right and left alternately	5
	• The player combines the elements of the above drills (thigh, head and foot) in a given sequence: <foot – head> <foot – thigh> <thigh – head> <foot – thigh- head>	5
SOCCER TENNIS WITHOUT A NET 	**Rules of the game:** • Two players are on a pitch measuring 5 x 5 yards. • A serves the ball into play, sending it at least above head height. • The ball may only bounce once and must reach at least head height. • Each player can only touch the ball once, with head, foot or thigh. • If the ball lands outside of the pitch, the other player serves. • If a player makes a mistake the other wins a point. • A game lasts until 15 points are scored or until a certain time has passed (e.g. 3-5 minutes).	35

Practice Session no. 11
Juggling 2

ORGANIZATION	DESCRIPTION	TIME
CROSS RUNS	• A group of players stands in line beside each of the four cones. • The players of groups A and B give the start signal. • Players A1 and C1 run toward the center cone, then B1 and D1 do the same. • The players adjust their speed so that they run around the center cone simultaneously and turn through 90 degrees. **Variations:** • The players turn through 180 degrees. • All four players start simultaneously. • The players run sideways or hop or run backward toward the center cone	15
STRETCHING EXERCISES		5
STANDING ON THE SPOT AND KICKING THE BALL INTO THE AIR WITH THE INSTEP	**Drill 1:** The player throws the ball up with both hands. As it falls he kicks it straight back up into the air with his instep (right or left or right and left alternately) and catches it. **Drill 2:** Gradually he reduces the height of the kick into the air. **Drill 3:** He kicks the ball high into the air, allows it to bounce, kicks it into the air again and catches it. **Drill 4:** Each time the ball bounces, the player kicks it into the air with his instep. **Drill 5:** He tries to kick the ball into the air several times in succession without allowing it to bounce.	10

ORGANIZATION	DESCRIPTION	TIME
MOVING FORWARD AND KICKING THE BALL INTO THE AIR WITH THE INSTEP	**Drill 6:** The player kicks the ball into the air with his instep as he moves forward.	5
SEQUENCE: INSTEP-FOREHEAD-GROUND	**Drill 7:** The player kicks the ball up with his instep so that he can head it. He allows the headed ball to bounce and volleys it up again with his instep so that he can head it again.	10
INSTEP, HEAD, CHEST, THIGH	**Drill 8:** The player juggles the ball, using his instep, head, chest and thigh to keep the ball in the air for as long as possible. If the ball falls to the ground, he lifts it with his foot (as in drill 9).	10
USING THE FOOT TO LIFT THE BALL OFF THE GROUND	**Drill 9:** The ball is on the ground. The player rolls it back with the sole of his shoe, places his instep under the ball and lifts it quickly off the ground. He can then flip or kick the ball into the air and juggle it.	5

ORGANIZATION	DESCRIPTION	TIME
DRIBBLERS V JUGGLERS: 	**Rules of the game:** • The coach forms two equal teams. • The coach gives the start signal. All of the players of team A dribble round a square with sides measuring 10 yards long. • On the start signal the first player of team B starts to juggle with a ball. Each ball contact (foot, thigh, head) scores one point. • The ball can touch the ground, but the player must not use his hands to lift it up again. • When the last dribbler crosses the finishing line the coach stops counting the juggler's ball contacts. • After the first dribbling circuits (depending on the size of the teams) the teams swap roles, so that the dribblers can have a period of rest. • Each player should juggle once. If the teams have unequal numbers the coach selects one player to juggle twice. • The winner is the team that achieves the most ball contacts. **Variation:** If more counters are available, more jugglers can start simultaneously.	20

Practice Session no. 12
Juggling 3

ORGANIZATION	DESCRIPTION	TIME
CAR RACE – A GAME WITHOUT A WINNER 	• The coach places cones to form a circle. This is important, as it gives the players a target to run to. • One player stands in the middle and the others stand around the edge of the circle (distance between players 6 to 12 yards, depending on the size of the group). • The coach goes from player to player and gives each one the name of a car company to remember, e.g. BMW, Mercedes (M), Porsche (P). • Each player is given a ball and dribbles to another cone when his car company name is called out. Fast reactions are required. • On the call "car race," all of the players have to change places but must not return to their own cone. • The player who is left without a cone calls out the next car company name or "car race".	15 5
STRETCHING EXERCISES		5
TWO PLAYERS KICK THE BALL TO EACH OTHER WITH THE INSTEP 	**Drill 1:** Two players stand facing each other 3 yards apart and kick the ball back and forth with the instep. The ball is controlled with the thigh, the chest or the head. The players then pick the ball up before kicking it with the instep.	5

ORGANIZATION	DESCRIPTION	TIME
	Drill 2: The players kick the ball back and forth with the instep. The ball is controlled with the thigh or the chest. They try to avoid using their hands.	5
	Two balls at the same time.	5
	Juggling and turning	5
	Juggling team Control the ball and play it to the other side.	5

ORGANIZATION	DESCRIPTION	TIME
	Play the ball around the circle. One player is in the center.	5
FINAL GAME: **TWO EQUAL TEAMS**	**Aims:** • Fast combinations with two ball contacts (control the ball with the first touch and pass or shoot with the second). • Show confident ball control in a game situation.	5

Practice Session no. 13
Shooting 1

ORGANIZATION	DESCRIPTION	TIME
ISLAND HOPPING	• Islands (tires, squares of four cones) are spread around the playing area. • The players dribble the ball at random around the playing area. • When the coach whistles or calls, the players dribble as fast as they can to the nearest island. • No more than two players can occupy one island. • Players who fail to find an island score one minus point. • The player with the fewest minus points wins.	15
STRETCHING EXERCISES		5
	Shooting technique • Straight run up. • Standing leg to the side of the ball, around a foot's width away from it. • Toes of the standing leg pointing at the target. • Draw back the kicking leg, bending the knee, and swing the leg forward in a straight line. • Toes of the kicking foot pointing down. • Keep the ankle rigid. • After kicking the ball, continue the leg's forward swing (follow through).	10

ORGANIZATION	DESCRIPTION	TIME
SHOOTING AT TWO GOALS (GROUP OF FOUR PLAYERS)	• Two teams of two players (A is the goalkeeper and B stands 5 to 7 yards behind the goal and fetches the ball when it passes the goal. • The goalkeepers shoot alternately at the opposing goal. • They can try to score from rebounds. • After 3 minutes the players swap roles. (Fetcher becomes goalkeeper and goalkeeper becomes fetcher).	10
FIRST-TIME SHOT FROM A PASS	• The passer (A) stands near the goal. • The striker (B) is behind the shooting line, around 10 yards in front of the goal. • The goalkeeper (C) is in the goal and a fetcher (D) is behind the goal. • A passes to B, who shoots first time. He can try to score from a rebound. • All balls are returned to A. • After 10 passes the players swap roles. • Who scores the most goals?	10
FIRST-TIME SHOT ON THE TURN	• As above. • B runs onto the pass from the side and shoots first-time on the turn.	

ORGANIZATION	DESCRIPTION	TIME
LOWBALL	**Rules of the game:**	20
	• The playing area is divided into three sections.	
	• In the middle zone are the goalkeepers, who are chosen by the coach.	
	• The players in the two end zones have to kick the ball low (no higher than hip height) past the goalkeepers as often as possible.	
	• Each time that a player kicks the ball through the middle zone to the opposite end zone he scores a point.	
	• When a goalkeeper stops a shot, he swaps places with the kicker.	
	• The player who scores the most points wins.	

Practice Session no. 14
Shooting 1

ORGANIZATION	DESCRIPTION	TIME
SHIELDING THE BALL 	**Rules of the game:** • Four players, each with a ball, dribble around the playing area, shielding the ball from the ball thieves. • The ball thieves follow the dribblers and try to kick the ball out of play if the opportunity arises. • If a player has to leave the playing area to fetch his ball, he scores one minus point. • The player with the fewest minus points wins the game.	15
STRETCHING EXERCISES		5
SHOOTING AT TWO GOALS (GROUP OF FOUR PLAYERS) 	• Two teams of two players. The teams attack and defend alternately. • One player of the attacking team passes the ball diagonally into the shooting zone. • The striker controls the ball and shoots at the goal. • After each shot the teams swap roles. The goalkeeper becomes the striker and the fetcher becomes the passer. • After a team has made 5 attacks, the two players swap roles.	10

ORGANIZATION	DESCRIPTION	TIME
SHOOTING AT TWO GOALS (GROUP OF FOUR PLAYERS)	• As in the previous diagram. • The striker always starts from the goal line. • A goal only counts if the striker shoots from the goal zone.	10
PASS AND SHOOT	• Each team has two players. The teams attack and defend alternately. • In the middle zone (shooting zone) is a neutral player (M). • The striker plays the ball low to M, who plays a return pass so that the striker can shoot at the defending team's goal. • The teams swap roles. The goalkeeper now becomes the striker. He passes the ball to M, etc. • After 10 shots the players swap roles.	10
	• As above • The ball is now played diagonally to the striker.	

ORGANIZATION	DESCRIPTION	TIME
LONG SHOTS 	• In each half of the playing area are three players and a goalkeeper. • Players can only score goals by shooting from their own half. • The players are not allowed to cross the center line.	20

Practice Session no. 15
Heading 1

ORGANIZATION	DESCRIPTION	TIME
WARMING UP (GROUP OF FIVE PLAYERS) 	Five players stand in a circle and head a ball to each other. Beginners can catch the ball first, then throw it up and head it to the next player.	15
STRETCHING EXERCISES		5
HEADING FROM A STANDING POSITION 	• The players stand 3 to 5 yards apart. • A throws the ball up and heads it to B. • B catches the ball and heads it back in the same way. **Note:** • The more practice the players have had, the further they should stand apart.	5
HEADING FROM A SITTING POSITION 	• The players sit 3 to 5 yards apart. • A throws the ball up and heads it from a sitting position to B. • B catches the ball and heads it back to A.	5

ORGANIZATION	DESCRIPTION	TIME
	Note: • The execution of the header is hampered by being in the sitting position. To impart more momentum to the ball the players have to lean the upper body backward and then jerk forward to head the ball. • This drill should only be carried out on a dry, warm surface.	10
HEADING THE BALL BACK TO THE THROWER	• A throws the ball to B • B heads the ball back to A so that A can catch it. **Note:** • After 5 throws the players swap roles. **Variation:** The players try to head the ball back and forth ten times.	5
HEADING WHILE MOVING FORWARD	• A moves back and throws the ball to B. • B runs forward and heads the ball back to B so that B can catch it. • After covering 10 to 15 yards the players swap roles and repeat the drill in the opposite direction.	5
FINAL GAME: **HANDBALL-HEADBALL**	**Rules of the game:** • Two teams and two goals. • The players throw the ball to each other. • Goals can only be scored with headers.	30

Practice Session no. 16
Heading 2

ORGANIZATION	DESCRIPTION	TIME
HARES AND FOXES	• Each hare has a ball and dribbles randomly in the playing area. • Depending on the number of players, there are two to four foxes. Each of them holds a ball. • The foxes have to chase the hares, throwing their ball into the air and trying to head it against a hare. • If a hare is hit by a fox's ball, he scores a minus point. • When a hare is hit, he picks up his ball and becomes a fox. • The winner is the player with the fewest minus points after 15 minutes	15
STRETCHING EXERCISES		5
HEADING ON THE TURN – FROM A STANDING POSITION	• A throws the ball to B and runs to the side. • B heads the ball on the turn so that it returns to A, who catches it. • After 5 headers the players swap roles. **Note:** • B should turn his upper body toward A before heading the ball.	5

ORGANIZATION	DESCRIPTION	TIME
HEADING ON THE TURN – WHILE ON THE	• A throws the ball up high so that it falls to one side of B. • B runs to the side and heads the ball back on the turn. • After 5 throws the players swap roles. **Note:** • The more practice the players have had, the further to the side the ball can be thrown.	5
c) HEADING WHILE MOVING FORWARD	• The players run forward in parallel, 3 to 5 yards apart. • A throws the ball into B's path. • B heads the ball back into A's path so that A can catch it. • A catches the ball and throws it into B's path again. This sequence is repeated until the players have covered the given distance (around 20 yards).	10
FINAL GAME: "FROM GOAL TO GOAL"	**Rules of the game:** • Two goals are set up 3 to 7 yards apart. • A throws the ball from the goal line to B. • B tries to head the ball directly into A's goal. If he does so, he scores a point. • The height of the goals is the same as the height of the players. **Note:** • The ball must be thrown in such a way that the other player can head it easily.	30

Practice Session no. 17
Heading 3

ORGANIZATION	DESCRIPTION	TIME
5 v 2 	• Five players on the outside pass the ball to each other so precisely that the two players in the middle cannot reach the ball. • The players in the middle challenge in a coordinated manner and wait for an outside player to make a mistake. • When an outside player makes a mistake, he swaps places with the midfield player who has been in the middle longest.	15
STRETCHING EXERCISES		5
HEADING (GROUPS OF THREE) **A) 2 BALLS – SLIGHT TURN** 	• A and B each have a ball. They throw alternately to C, who heads the ball back to the thrower so that the thrower can catch it. **Variation:** • A and B move backward and C heads the ball as he moves forward.	5

ORGANIZATION	DESCRIPTION	TIME
B) 2 BALLS – 180-DEGREE TURN 	• A, B and C stand in a line • A and B hold a ball. • C is in the middle between A and B. • A throws the ball to C, who heads it back and immediately turns to face B. • B throws the ball and C heads it back. • After 10 headers the players swap roles. **Variation:** A and B throw the ball up in the air and head it to C	5
C) 1 BALL – B AND C CHANGE 	• A, B and C stand in a line • A and B hold a ball. • A is the permanent thrower. • A throws the ball to B, who heads it back then swaps places with C. A throws the ball to C, who heads it back and swaps places with B, and so on.	5
D) 1 BALL – CHANGE OF TASKS	• A throws to B, who heads to C. • C catches the ball and throws to A, who heads to B. • B catches the ball and throws to C, who heads it to A. • And so on.	30

ORGANIZATION	DESCRIPTION	TIME
FINAL GAME – HEADHUNTING 	**Rules of the game:** • Three hunters are in each outside zone. • Three foxes are on the ground in the center zone. • A hunter holds a ball and throws it over the center zone. • A player of the group at the other end heads it at a fox. • If he succeeds in hitting the fox, the hunter scores a point. • If he misses, he swaps places with the fox he aimed at. • The fox stands up and takes the hunter's place. • The players in the center zone can only try to avoid being hit by crawling on all fours, rolling away or lying on their stomach.	30

Practice Session no. 18
Heading 4

ORGANIZATION	DESCRIPTION	TIME
CHARACTERISTICS: 	All of the players dribble at random around the playing area. The coach calls out a characteristic and all of the players who have this characteristic become catchers. Who catches the most players within 15 minutes? Examples of characteristics that might be used: • Color of the players' overvests • Hair color • Color of the players' tee shirts • First letter of the players' names **Note:** It is important that the characteristic should be easily understandable. The coach should give everyone an equal chance of becoming a catcher.	15
STRETCHING EXERCISES		5
HEADING (GROUP OF THREE) 	• The header (B) stands around 6 to 8 yards in front of the goal. • The thrower (A) stands to the side of the goal. He lobs the ball in such a way that the header has to run to meet it. • A heads the ball at goal while on the run. • D fetches the balls that get beyond the goal.	5

ORGANIZATION	DESCRIPTION	TIME
	• The thrower (A) stands a few yards from the goal, to one side of it. • He lobs the ball to the header in such a way that the header has to run diagonally to meet it.	10
	• The thrower is behind the header and lobs the ball forward diagonally. • The header heads the ball on the turn toward the goal from a standing position.	10
FINAL GAME: FROM GOAL TO GOAL 	**Rules of the game:** • Two goals are set up 4 to 7 yards apart. • Player A stands on one goal line. He throws the ball into the air and tries to head it into the other goal. • The height of the goals is the same as the height of the players. • Each goal counts as one point. **Notes:** • The coach organizes a small tournament. • Each player plays five times against different players, who are chosen by the coach. • The playing time is 5 minutes. • The changeover interval is one minute. • Three points are awarded for a win and 1 point for a draw.	30

Practice Session no. 19
Heading 5

ORGANIZATION	DESCRIPTION	TIME
WARMING UP: 	Players A, B and C run clockwise in a circle around D. D throws the ball to A, B and C in succession. They head the ball back so that D can catch it. After 9 headers the players turn around and run counterclockwise. After another 9 headers an outside player swaps with the player in the middle.	7
	As before, but now the players run after the ball and take the place of the player they headed it to.	8
STRETCHING EXERCISES		5

ORGANIZATION	DESCRIPTION	TIME
	Header – shot: Two players build up an attack from their own goal line by throwing the ball up and heading it to each other in turn. At the other end of the playing area they try to head the ball into the goal. The last player throws the ball up and tries to head it into goal himself. After each header at goal the teams swap roles.	10
SEE HEADER SHOT ABOVE	A goal only counts if the header goes into goal directly.	10

ORGANIZATION	DESCRIPTION	TIME
	The players can catch the ball and head it, or head it without first catching it. Goals only count if they are scored directly.	10
	Rules of the game: • A cord is fixed across the playing area at a height of one yard. The center line can also be marked with two cones. • The first player throws the ball up and heads it into the opposition's half. • The defending team must not let the ball touch the ground, otherwise the opposition is awarded a point. • If the ball goes directly to ground in the opposition's half after a header, two points are awarded. **Variation:** The ball is thrown by a teammate before being headed into the other half.	30

Practice Session no. 20
Goalkeeper 1

ORGANIZATION	DESCRIPTION	TIME
THROWING AND CATCHING		
	• The goalkeeper throws the ball in the air and catches it again from standing, sitting and kneeling positions, then when moving forward, backward or sideways and while sprinting. • He uses both hands to throw and catch the ball. • He throws the ball with one hand and catches it with both hands. • He throws the ball as high as he can.	10
BOUNCING		
	• The goalkeeper stands with his feet slightly apart. • He bounces the ball one-handed around his body. • He changes hands in front of and behind his body.	5
STRETCHING EXERCISES		5
	• The goalkeeper throws the ball up and catches it at head height.	5

ORGANIZATION	DESCRIPTION	TIME
CATCHING THE BALL AT HIP HEIGHT 	• The goalkeeper stands 1 to 2 yards away from the coach, who throws the ball to him. • The coach throws the ball from a distance of 4 to 5 yards. • The coach kicks the ball to the goalkeeper from a distance of 8 to 10 yards. • The coach lobs the ball up from a distance of 6 to 8 yards so that it bounces in front of the goalkeeper. The goalkeeper walks forward initially, then runs and gathers the ball on the run.	10
LIFTING THE BALL FROM THE GROUND TO FULL STRETCH ABOVE THE HEAD 	• The ball lies on the ground in front of the goalkeeper. The goalkeeper bends forward, picks up the ball and lifts it at full stretch above his head before putting it down again.	5
	• The goalkeeper holds the ball level with his forehead, with his arms slightly bent. He pushes the ball 1 to 1.5 feet into the air and catches it again. • The goalkeeper throws the ball 1 to 2 yards into the air and catches it again.	5

ORGANIZATION	DESCRIPTION	TIME
CIRCLE GAME:	**Rules of the game** • The goalkeepers face each other on opposite sides of a circle. Goalkeeper A holds the ball. • Goalkeeper A serves the ball by throwing it one- or two-handed across the circle. The ball must bounce in the circle. • Goalkeeper B moves toward the ball and tries to catch it. • If goalkeeper B catches the ball, he becomes the server and throws the ball back across the circle again, bouncing it in the circle. If goalkeeper B fails to catch the ball, however, goalkeeper A serves again. • If the throw bounces outside rather than inside the circle, the service changes hands. **Scoring points** • The server scores a point if the receiver fails to catch the throw, and the receiver scores a point if the server bounces the ball outside of the circle. • Which goalkeeper scores the most points in a given time? **Variations** • The ball may only be caught and thrown with the same hand. • Enlarge or shrink the diameter of the circle.	10

Practice Session no. 21
Goalkeeper 2

ORGANIZATION	DESCRIPTION	TIME
THROWING AND CATCHING	• From a standing position, the goalkeeper throws the ball one-handed into air and catches it. • He throws and catches the ball with his right (or left) hand. (diagram) • He throws the ball with his right (or left) hand and catches it with his left (or right) hand.	7
BOUNCING	• The goalkeeper bounces the ball one-handed while moving forward, backward or sideways. (diagram) • The goalkeeper bounces the ball with only one hand while he runs. He repeatedly varies his speed and direction.	8
ROLLING	• The goalkeeper rolls the ball with one hand, keeping his fingertips in contact with the ball. • He runs sideways or backward. • He increases his speed. • He repeatedly varies his speed and direction. • The goalkeeper changes hands repeatedly as he rolls the ball forward.	5
STRETCHING		5

ORGANIZATION	DESCRIPTION	TIME
PICKING UP THE BALL FROM THE GROUND	• The goalkeeper picks up the stationary ball from a standing position and gathers it to his chest.	5
	• The goalkeeper moves toward the stationary ball, then stops, picks it up and gathers it to his chest.	5
	• The coach rolls the ball slowly to the goalkeeper, who picks it up and gathers it to his chest. (diagram) • The coach rolls the ball slowly to the goalkeeper, who moves to meet it, then picks it up and gathers it to his chest.	5
	• The coach kicks the ball to the goalkeeper, who picks it up and gathers it to his chest from a standing position and then as he moves to meet it.	5
	• The coach plays the ball to the goalkeeper from a distance of 1 to 2 yards. • The goalkeeper picks the ball up from a standing position, then after moving forward and taking a quick step to the side.	5

ORGANIZATION	DESCRIPTION	TIME
"THROWING AT GOAL" 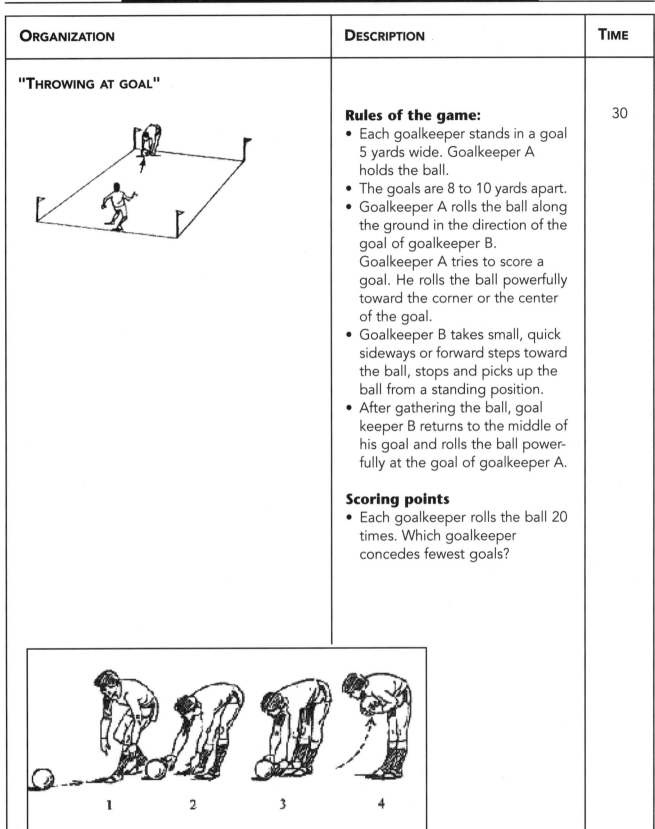	**Rules of the game:** • Each goalkeeper stands in a goal 5 yards wide. Goalkeeper A holds the ball. • The goals are 8 to 10 yards apart. • Goalkeeper A rolls the ball along the ground in the direction of the goal of goalkeeper B. Goalkeeper A tries to score a goal. He rolls the ball powerfully toward the corner or the center of the goal. • Goalkeeper B takes small, quick sideways or forward steps toward the ball, stops and picks up the ball from a standing position. • After gathering the ball, goal keeper B returns to the middle of his goal and rolls the ball powerfully at the goal of goalkeeper A. **Scoring points** • Each goalkeeper rolls the ball 20 times. Which goalkeeper concedes fewest goals?	30

Practice Session no. 22
Goalkeeper 2

ORGANIZATION	DESCRIPTION	TIME
THROWING AND CATCHING	• The goalkeeper throws the ball in the air from a standing position and catches it again. • After the goalkeeper throws the ball up he makes a complete turn. • The goalkeeper sits down and then quickly jumps to his feet again. • After the goalkeeper throws the ball up he touches the ground with both hands. • The goalkeeper kneels down and then jumps quickly to his feet again.	10
BOUNCING	• While bouncing the ball with his right (or left) hand, the goalkeeper rises from a lying position to a kneeling position, then squats and then stands. • He then slowly returns to the lying position, this time bouncing the ball with his left (or right) hand.	5
ROLLING	• The goalkeeper rolls the ball forward with one hand. • His fingertips remain in contact with the ball. • The goalkeeper rolls the ball in small and large circles, a zigzag, a figure of eight and a slalom with just one hand or changing hands at intervals.	5
STRETCHING		5

ORGANIZATION	DESCRIPTION	TIME
ROLLING TO THE SIDE	• The goalkeeper lies on his side with his calf, thigh, hip and shoulder touching the ground. • The coach rolls the ball at the goalkeeper's body. The goalkeeper gathers the ball to his body with both hands. • The coach rolls the ball close to the goalkeeper's head. The goalkeeper stretches his arms and grasps the ball. The hand of the lower arm should be positioned under and behind the ball and the hand of the upper arm should be positioned on top and behind it.	5
	• The goalkeeper kneels, keeping his upper body erect. • The coach throws the ball to him slightly above head height. The goalkeeper catches the ball, gathers it to his body and rolls to the side. • The coach throws the ball slightly to the side of the goalkeeper. The goal-keeper stretches his arms to reach the ball, catches it and gathers it to his body.	5
	• The coach rolls the ball to the side of the goalkeeper but within his reach. The goalkeeper rolls to the side, grasps the ball and gathers it to his body.	5

ORGANIZATION	DESCRIPTION	TIME
	• The goalkeeper is in a squatting position. He saves the ball without taking both feet off the ground. • He tries to gather the ball to his body as quickly as possible. • The coach throws the ball at shoulder height or higher, within reach of the goalkeeper.	5
	• The coach throws the ball to the side of the goalkeeper at a height of 6 inches to 2 feet. • The coach rolls the ball to the side of the goalkeeper but within his reach.	5
	• The coach kicks the ball low to the side of the goalkeeper but within his reach. • He gradually kicks the ball harder.	5
"GATHERING THE BALL AFTER IT BOUNCES" 10 yds 10 yds	• 2 goalkeepers stand in a square playing area with sides 10 yards long. • Goalkeeper A holds the ball. **Rules of the game** • Goalkeeper A throws the ball high into the air so that it falls inside the playing area. • Goalkeeper B runs toward the ball and tries to gather it after it bounces. • After goalkeeper A has thrown the	5

ORGANIZATION	DESCRIPTION	TIME
	ball up 5 times the players swap roles. **Scoring points** • A point is scored if the ball falls outside of the playing area or bounces more than once inside the playing area or is not thrown above head height. • The goalkeeper who scores 21 points first is the winner.	

Practice Session no. 23
Goalkeeper 4

ORGANIZATION	DESCRIPTION	TIME
THROWING AND CATCHING 	• Each goalkeeper has a ball. They throw the balls two-handed to each other and catch them. • The goalkeepers stand, sit or kneel 3 yards apart. • The goalkeepers throw the balls to each other from constantly changing distances.	10
BOUNCING 	• The goalkeepers bounce the ball to each other while moving forward, backward or sideways, changing direction constantly. • The distance between the goalkeepers can be increased or decreased. The ball must not bounce more than once.	5

ORGANIZATION	DESCRIPTION	TIME
ROLLING	• The goalkeepers stand 3 yards apart. • They bend forward and roll the ball one-handed to each other. • Both goalkeepers roll the ball with only the right or left hand. • Goalkeeper A rolls the ball with the left (or right) hand, while goalkeeper B uses the right (or left) hand.	5
STRETCHING		5
	• The goalkeeper is in a squatting position. He leaps to the ball, catches it and gathers it to his body as he lands. • The coach throws the ball at shoulder height or higher, but within reach, to the side of the goalkeeper.	5
	• The coach kicks the ball low, with gradually increasing force, 2 to 3 yards to the side of the goalkeeper, but within his reach.	5

ORGANIZATION	DESCRIPTION	TIME
FINAL GAME "BASELINERS" 	The playing area is marked by 4 flags. It is 20 yards long and 8 yards wide and is divided in two by a center line. In each half of the playing area is a goalkeeper. Goalkeeper A holds a ball. **Rules of the game** • Goalkeeper A throws the ball into goalkeeper B's half. • He tries to throw the ball over goalkeeper B's baseline. • Goalkeeper B tries to prevent the ball from crossing his baseline. • The ball must not be thrown higher than the goalkeeper can reach. • If the ball is thrown too high, the throw is invalid and the players swap roles. • If the ball touches the ground inside goalkeeper B's half, goalkeeper B throws it back from the point where it touched. • Goalkeeper B can move forward 3 steps before throwing the ball back if he manages to catch the ball. • The goalkeepers must not cross the center line. • If the ball crosses the sideline, the next throw is taken from the place where the ball crossed the line. **Scoring points** • If the ball crosses the opponent's baseline, the thrower scores a point. • Which goalkeeper scores the most points in a given time?	35

Practice Session no. 24
Coordination

ORGANIZATION	DESCRIPTION	TIME
WARMING UP	The players dribble with different balls (soccer ball, softball, rubber ball, water ball, tennis ball) and carry out various tasks: • Dribbling fast and slow • Turning through large and small circles, using the inside and the outside of the foot (turning counter clockwise and clockwise) • Stopping the ball when the coach makes a signal • Kicking the ball 5 yards away and catching it • Carry out feints (step-over, scissor, drag-back, etc.)	15
STRETCHING EXERCISES		5
DRILLS WITH RODS	A number of coordination drills belong to the warming-up part of this practice session: **Tasks:** • Run over the rods – right foot first – three steps in the middle • Run over the rods – left foot first – three steps in the middle • After crossing all the rods, sprint 10 yards	5
	Tasks: • Slalom (ball in hand) through the rods • Dribble through the rods	5

ORGANIZATION	DESCRIPTION	TIME
	Tasks: • Sprint over the rods (ball in hand) • Throw the ball on the ground and shoot at the goal.	5
	Jumping Jacks in tire circuit (opening and closing the legs) **Arm movements:** • up - down • left arm forward – right arm forward	5
	Jumping Jacks with turn in the middle Fast orientation!	5
CATCH THE DRIBBLER 	**Rules of the game:** • A team of dribblers plays against a team of field players. • The dribblers stand behind the starting line (e.g. the goal line) with a ball. • The first dribbler has a second ball. He kicks off the game by kicking the ball as far as he can into the playing area. • He and his teammates then dribble as fast as they can to the turning point and try to reach the finishing line before the field team can score a goal. • The field team is awarded a point for each dribbler who fails to reach the finishing line before the field team scores. • After each player on the dribbling team has kicked off, the teams swap roles. • The field team becomes the dribbling team and vice versa.	30

- The team that scores the most points wins.

Note:
The coach should place the turning point for the dribblers in such a way that both teams have a fair chance of winning. If all of the dribblers always reach the finishing line the distance is too short. If the dribblers have no chance of reaching the finishing line, the turning point is too far away.

**#788 Zone Play: A
Tactical and
Technical Handbook**
Pereni and Di Cesare
$14.95

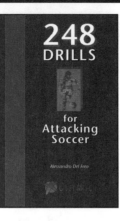

**#794 248 Drills for
Attacking Soccer**
by Allessandro Del Freo
$14.95

#154 Coaching Soccer
by Bert van Lingen
$14.95

**#261 Match Analysis
and Game
Preparation**
*by Kormelink and
Seeverens*
$12.95

**#177 Principles of
Brazilian Soccer**
*by Jose' Thadeu
Goncalves*
$16.95

**#175 The Coaching
Philosophies of Louis
van Gaal and the
Ajax Coaches**
*by Kormelink and
Seeverens*
$14.95

**#785 Complete Book
of Soccer Restart
Plays**
*by Mario Bonfanti and
Angelo Pereni*
$14.95

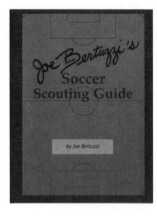

**#789 Soccer Scouting
Guide**
by Joe Bertuzzi
$12.95

REEDSWAIN
612 Pughtown Road • Spring City PA 19475
1-800-331-5191 • www.reedswain.com

#765 Attacking Schemes and Training Exercises
by Fascetti and Scaia
$14.95

#185 Conditioning for Soccer
Dr. Raymond Verheijen
$19.95

#786 Soccer Nutrition
by Enrico Arcelli
$10.95

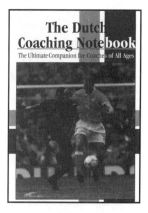

#284 The Dutch Coaching Notebook
$14.95

#244 Coaching the 4-4-2
by Marziali and Mora
$14.95

#291 Soccer Fitness Training *by Enrico Arcelli and Ferretto Ferretti*
$12.95

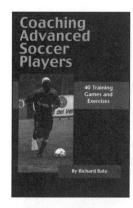

#169 Coaching Advanced Soccer Players
by Richard Bate
$12.95

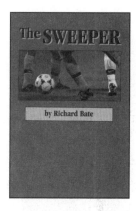

#225 The Sweeper
by Richard Bate
$9.95

REEDSWAIN
612 Pughtown Road • Spring City PA 19475
1-800-331-5191 • www.reedswain.com

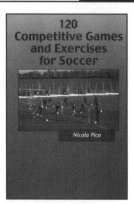

#792 120 Competitive Games and Exercises for Soccer
by Nicola Pica
$14.95

#256 The Creative Dribbler
by Peter Schreiner
$14.95

#267 Developing Soccer Players The Dutch Way
$12.95

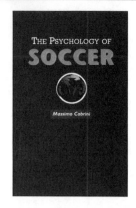

#262 Psychology of Soccer
by Massimo Cabrini
$12.95

#287 Team Building
by Kormelink and Seeverens
$9.95

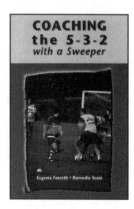

#793 Coaching the 5-3-2 with a Sweeper
by Fascetti and Scaia
$14.95

#167 Soccer Training Games, Drills and Fitness Practices
by Malcolm Cook
$14.95

#905 Soccer Strategies: Defensive and Attacking Tactics
by Robyn Jones
$12.95

REEDSWAIN
612 Pughtown Road • Spring City PA 19475
1-800-331-5191 • www.reedswain.com

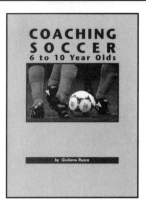

**#264 Coaching Soccer
6 to 10 year Olds**
by Giuliano Rusca
$14.95

**#195
Dutch Soccer Drills Vol. 3**
by Henny Kormelink
$12.95

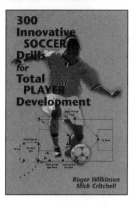

**#188 300 Innovative
SOCCER Drills for
Total PLAYER
Development**
*by Roger Wilkinson
and Mick Critchell*
$14.95

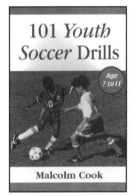

**#254   101 Youth
Soccer Drills
Ages 7-11**
by Malcolm Cook
$14.95

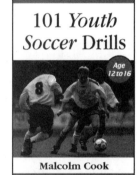

**#255   101 Youth
Soccer Drills
Ages 12-16**
by Malcolm Cook
$14.95

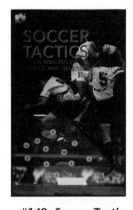

**#149 Soccer Tactics
An Analysis of Attack
and Defense**
by Massimo Lucchesi
$12.95

**#249 Coaching the
3-4-3**
by Massimo Lucchesi
$12.95

**#161 Goalkeeping
Drills
Volume One**
*by
Gerd Thissen
Klaus Röllgen*
$12.95

**#162 Goalkeeping
Drills
Volume Two**
*by
Gerd Thissen
Klaus Röllgen*
$12.95

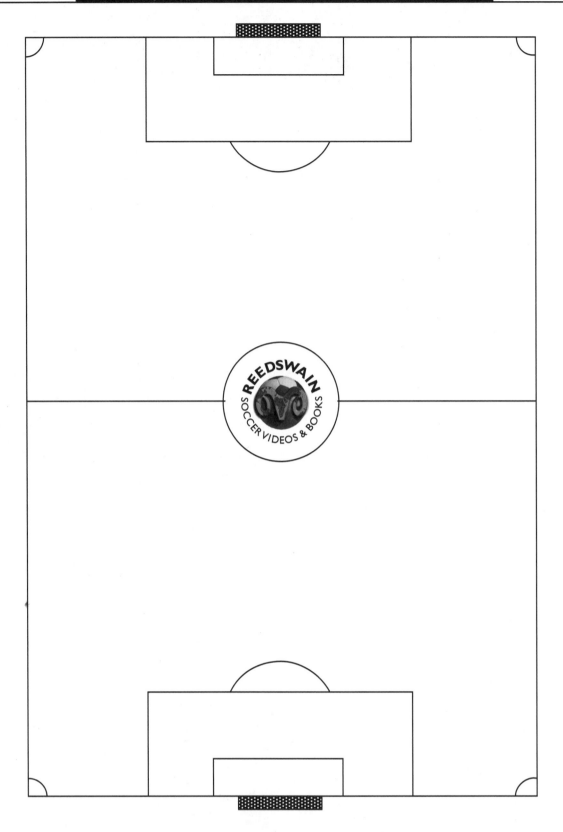

REEDSWAIN
612 Pughtown Road • Spring City PA 19475
1-800-331-5191 • www.reedswain.com